T0193265

FACTUAL
OR
ACTUAL?

THE DIFFERENCE BETWEEN
INTELLECTUAL ACKNOWLEDGMENT AND GENUINE FAITH

MATTHEW BRADEN

WESTBOW
PRESS®
A DIVISION OF THOMAS NELSON
& ZONDERVAN

WestBow Press books may be ordered through booksellers or by contacting:

WestBow Press
A Division of Thomas Nelson & Zondervan
1663 Liberty Drive
Bloomington, IN 47403
www.westbowpress.com
844-714-3454

ISBN: 978-1-6642-7532-4 (sc)
ISBN: 978-1-6642-7533-1 (hc)
ISBN: 978-1-6642-7531-7 (e)

Library of Congress Control Number: 2022915033

Print information available on the last page.

WestBow Press rev. date: 09/09/2022

CONTENTS

FOREWORD

In Mark's gospel, we read a strange account of a certain young man. The young man was a timid follower of Jesus. He, like the eleven apostles, took flight when Jesus was arrested. However, unlike the eleven apostles, this one had a sheet wrapped around his naked body. When those who arrested Jesus grabbed the young man by the blanket, he fled away naked (Mark 14:51–52).

Blankets are meant to bring us comfort and security. Clichés do the same thing. Even non-Christians take a false comfort in certain Christian clichés. The clichés, like our false blankets, will prove to be inadequate on the day when we face Him who has eyes as a flame of fire (Revelation 1:14). The day of judgment before the Christ who sits on the throne will unravel our false security and cloaks of deception. We, like the young man in Mark's account, might find ourselves naked. However, why wait for that day? How much better it is to see the real Jesus in the gospels, to hear His frightening warnings, and examine whether we are clothed with His righteous garment instead of our own blankets of false assurance.

Matthew Braden helps us to examine ourselves to see the real Jesus, the real gospel, and authentic discipleship. He carefully puts before the reader his own journey of faith. He offers introspective questions, which are not meant to make one feel uncomfortable for discomfort's sake, but serve as a warning and encouragement to make sure we know the real Jesus and not the façade of clichés and false blankets of self-deception.

Matthew then takes us to the next step: spiritual maturity and readiness, and spiritual warfare against the Devil's deception. Practical steps are demonstrated with appropriate and helpful Scripture. Matthew encourages the reader to make sure his faith is authentic and in the real Jesus. He offers strategies to deal with doubt and to face our insecurities, not with a false blanket but with the truth from the pages of the Bible. I highly encourage everyone to examine themselves in the light of eternity. To that end, you will find *Factual or Actual? The Difference between Intellectual Acknowledgment and Genuine Faith* a must read.

Pastor Keith Surland

PREFACE

This book discusses the difference between an intellectual, factual knowledge of the Scriptures (God's Word) and the actual change that occurs when the facts become more than just knowledge, more than a "Christianese" language, more than a culture or religion, and certainly more than a guarantee of heaven after death.

I grew up in a Christian home and attended almost every church event with my family, whether it was on a Sunday or any other day during the week. My parents started attending Mount Airy Bible Church before I was even born. I can truly say I have been going to this church my entire existence— from the time I was conceived all the way to the present day. My family, consisting of Mom, Dad, and my three siblings, always went to the early morning church service. My siblings and I would occasionally be smacked in the back of the head if we were not paying attention or singing along during service. We attended the AWANA program on Wednesday nights and went to every church picnic. We even helped with building or cleaning projects on the Saturday "work days" organized by the deacons.

When I was young, my parents decided to homeschool

my siblings and me so that they could instill in us a Biblical worldview and cultivate a work ethic pleasing to God. When high school rolled around, we were placed in our church's affiliated Christian school, Mount Airy Christian Academy, where we continued to learn more about the Bible and how to live as Christians.

At this time, I started to serve in the church myself. I served as a singer on the worship team, I started singing in youth group on Wednesdays, I helped with children's church, and I even worked as a handyman at church during the summer. I was very involved, served everywhere I could, and learned everything that I could about God.

That is the kind of Christian environment I grew up in. At the time, I thought my heart was in all of it. I remember one time when I was about twelve, I touched one of the windows at church with my hand. My dad sarcastically said, "Do you want to clean that window?" so that I would stop. I replied out of the sincerity of my heart that wanted to serve, "Sure!"

I was the kid who always wanted to have the right heart. I *wanted* to please God and serve Him in whatever way that I could. Throughout high school, I was called a "goody-two-shoes" because I would not participate in anything that I did not think would glorify God. I even started a guys' Bible study with a buddy of mine; it met once a week during lunch at school. I also received a perfect grade on my ten-step study of Jephthah's oath in Judges 11. My Bible teacher said, with raised eyebrows, "I couldn't find anything wrong with your study. I read it many times." And I drafted a stellar senior thesis on the proof of Christ's resurrection.

I say all these things not to puff myself up, but to prove my point. Out of all the kids in my graduating class at the Christian school, I was determined to be the one who would always follow God no matter what; who had a sincere heart; who would never stray; who turned his nose up at anyone who drank alcohol or went to parties; who hated cursing and would never do it. I was always angry when I heard the statistic that four out of five youths in the Church would leave after graduating high school. That was *not* going to be me—but it was.

After graduating from high school and becoming freer than I had ever been, the lies underneath the layers of my Christian living started to emerge and take over. Time slowly uncovered the reality that my "Christian" life was just a veil for the sin that held me captive. Over the span of two and a half years after graduating from high school, I became addicted to pornography, attended parties, drank alcohol and got drunk, messed around with a girl, and was involved in many other things. I became obsessed with my physical image. I watched horribly inappropriate movies and TV shows. I wasted thousands of dollars on my whims. I got a tattoo in defiance of my parents, and went to church only when I felt like it. In all of this, I thought that I was still trying to please God, and I still claimed Him to be my Savior. I was like those mentioned in Paul's letter to Titus.

> They profess to know God, but in works they deny Him, being abominable, disobedient, and disqualified for every good work. (Titus 1:16)

At this point in reading, you may be thinking, "Yeah, so what? I have done worse things than that. You just sound like the scared goody-two-shoes that you always were. Afraid to disobey your parents. Afraid to disappoint the big man upstairs." But that is just it—I was not afraid at all. I was comfortable justifying my actions based on my feelings, expecting that God would just forgive me afterwards (more on this later).

After two and a half years of rebellion, I woke up one morning and it was as if God had opened my eyes and showed me my life for what it really was: a life that denied Him. I was miserable. I was in pain. I was doing everything and anything that I wanted to do—yet I continued to come up empty. In pondering my misery, my mind kept returning to one question: "What does it mean to love God?" You see, I *claimed* to love Him, but my actions failed to show it. I had forgotten everything that I learned growing up. But that is just it; all I had done was learn the *facts*. And although I attempted to be changed by them, I never truly was. I never had the power in myself to do so. It is the Holy Spirit that makes the internal change, not us.

> Furthermore, just as they did not think it
> worthwhile to retain the knowledge of God,
> so God gave them over to a depraved mind,
> so that they do what ought not to be done.
> (Romans 1:28 NIV)

This book is written specifically for those who grew up within the church and know all the "right answers." God has placed this burden on my heart for those like me who grew up in the church but never, despite all efforts, understood the Gospel more than intellectually. However, this book holds truths from the Scriptures that apply to every person who is willing and wanting to grow in their faith. It is designed to challenge you to forget what you *think* you know, forget what any pastor or teacher has told you; to investigate the Word of God for yourself.

God's Word and the salvation that comes through Jesus Christ gives freedom from the lies and sin in our lives, not a Christian *fact* blanket to cover over them. Knowing Jesus intimately is more than knowing more and more *facts* about Him. Our reaction to those facts about who Jesus is and what it *actually* means for Him to love us and die for us creates an *actual* relationship of love with Him that overcomes all earthly circumstances and provides victory over sin. It is about meeting, for the first time, the *actual* person, Jesus—the relational *person*—rather than the *factual* distant being who created all things and wants us to live a certain way.

God has taught me through hard trials of crippling fear that "God has not given us a spirit of fear, but of power and of love and of a sound mind," and that He is greater than my inadequacies (2 Timothy 1:7). In fact, it is precisely our inadequacies that display God's greatness. For that reason, I will be sharing with you my many weaknesses, "that the power of Christ may rest upon me … For when I am weak, then I am strong" (2 Corinthians 12:9–10).

To God be all the glory for this book and for my life. I am one blade of grass amid a field of many others—no different than anyone else and deserving of eternal punishment. However,

Jesus has taken me from death unto life (John 5:24) and desires to do the same for you (2 Peter 3:9; 1 Timothy 2:3–4).

In preparing to write this book and throughout the process, I continued in prayer, surrendering all that I am to God and asking for guidance. The last thing that I want is to take God's Word out of context and use it to prove my own points. Rather, I desire with all my heart to present what the Bible declares, draw from it the eternal truths that God has made known to us, and share those truths with you.

ACKNOWLEDGMENT

I would like to express my sincere thanks to my wife Laura for all her support throughout the writing and editing process. She has been my chief encourager and supporter. She even helped me in the editing process to make the message of this book clear and direct, yet loving and full of grace. Thank you, Laura, for all your love and support.

Thanks to Ken and Kay Braden who have supported me in more ways than one and have made the publishing of this book possible. Without their love, support, and example, this book would not exist.

Special thanks also to the many who have prayed for and supported me throughout my life and in the writing and publishing of this book. There has been a passion within them for the message of this book to get out and impact those who need it.

Finally, I would like to thank God for all that He has done in my life and for how He has and is going to use the scrapes, bruises, and wounds of my life to help others to see *His* great love for them (2 Corinthians 1:3–4). He has been my best friend and has guided me through every trial, proving *Himself* faithful. I will continue to put my trust in Him for my life and future.

> To God be the glory great things He has done!
> So loved He the world that He gave us His Son,
> Who yielded His life an atonement for sin,
> And opened the life-gate that all may go in.
> Praise the Lord! Praise the Lord,
> Let the earth hear His voice!
> Praise the Lord! Praise the Lord!
> Let the people rejoice![1]

---

[1] Fanny Crosby, "To God Be the Glory," Hymnary.org, accessed February 20, 2022, https://hymnary.org/text/to_god_be_the_glory_great_things_he_hath.

HOW TO READ THIS BOOK

This book is intended to help readers see the difference between knowing God intellectually and knowing Him intimately. As Pastor Keith Surland, who authored the Foreword to this book, has said,

> This is not to say that knowing God intimately is devoid of an intellectual component. God has given to us reverent logic. But there *is* a danger in knowing theological precepts *without* knowing the God of the precepts.

Therefore, this book deals with the various reactions that people can have to the Gospel of Jesus Christ. The best way to read this book is to

1. **Look it up!** Open your Bible and place it next to this book. Search the Scriptures and view the truths for yourself. I have quoted many of the verses within the text, but have included many more references in parentheses for you to look up. It is a good habit to look up verses and passages *for yourself* to gain more

understanding and depth into the *context* of God's Word. Be a Berean (Acts 17:10–11).

2. **Put it down.** I would much sooner have you read and study God's Word than this book. The Bible is divinely inspired by God; this book is not. Therefore, do not use this as a substitute for time in the Word. This book is designed to inspire you to get into the Bible yourself. Allow the Holy Spirit to guide you. This book is simply a tool.

3. **Pray often.** When I read books, I often find myself pausing while reading to meditate on the truths that God is bringing to light in my life through the book. I encourage you to stop and thank God, praise God, confess to God, or whatever He is leading your heart to do. Stop reading and pray—wherever you are (Psalm 46:10).

4. **Ask and expect.** Ask God to lead you by the power of the Holy Spirit, and expect Him to do it as you read this book and as you read the Bible. God speaks to us through His Word, other believers, and His creation. Ask Him and He will answer. We just need to be sure that we are listening.

5. **Inter-Actual Exercise.** At the end of each chapter, there are reflective questions for you to think about as you *interact* with God in prayer. These questions will help you think through the implications of each chapter and what God has revealed to you through His Word.

CHAPTER 1

THE CHRISTIAN BLANKET

They profess to know God, but in works they deny Him, being abominable, disobedient, and disqualified for every good work.

—Titus 1:16

Growing up, I hated going to sleep without a blanket covering me. In my mind, it was the first line of defense. I felt that if I were under the blanket, no one could get me—no monster, no robber, no fire. I was completely protected if I was under that blanket. It covered every inch of my body—except my head (ironically one of the most important parts). Even on the hottest nights when I was sweating under the blanket, I kept it on top of me because I wanted to feel safe. You might ask, "Did you really think that a blanket would save you from harm?" Of course, I was young, and if you had asked me to think about it, I probably would have concluded that it would not stop a knife, a bullet, or a fire. But it gave me the *feeling* of safety, so I took cover underneath it every night.

Blankets are a great analogy to illustrate how many people

view Christianity, or religion in general. They want something to make them *feel* safe and covered, like a blanket. However, the truth will reveal that such blankets cannot do anything to save them or keep them from harm.

Unfortunately, many "Christians" today use Christianity as a blanket to cover themselves from any harm that may befall them. I put the name Christian in quotations because much of the time these blankets are used by those who call themselves Christians but do not know Jesus relationally. They have not surrendered their lives to Him. They have not been born again (John 3:3). I call the blanket they use "the Christian blanket."

AN AMERICAN LUXURY

The Christian blanket is an American luxury, like many other things in our country. It covers all who claim the name, it gives them eternal life, and—the best part—it allows them to live any way they want. Many people live like this, but can this really be what true, saving faith in Jesus Christ looks like? Or is it the love of self that drives this lifestyle?

The Christian blanket is provided in churches all around the country for free; however, in some cases, it requires a regular gift to the church and/or regular attendance. But this is a small price to pay for eternal security, right? If all I must do is go to church every week and occasionally drop whatever change I have on me into the offering basket, no problem. I can do that. I can even sing along with the band or choir and listen to the pastor (provided I can take a short snooze or send a text or two when things get uncomfortable or boring); if I am there, I am covered.

This is how some people, who call themselves Christians, act. They curse; take the name of the Lord in vain; watch, listen to, and indulge in worldly things all week; and sometimes are even nursing a hangover when they get to church on Sunday, if they even manage to show up. (These are all examples from my own life.) Some might even justify not going at all based on their preconceptions of the other attendees at the service. Maybe they often become bored, are offended, or can't get connected the way they think they should. So why go? They would like you to think that they still do their own study at home, but more than likely their Bible is collecting dust somewhere on a shelf. All this and still they steadily drag their Christian blanket around behind them, ready to claim the title in case the subject arises.

Strangely, the Christian blanket is not available internationally, since the price for claiming to be a Christian elsewhere is paid under the threat of persecution and even death. Just ask those in Nigeria, China, or Turkey if they know what the Christian blanket is. In these countries, the claim of being a Christian is hardly ever not followed by some form of severe maltreatment.

I often wonder where the mentality of the Christian blanket comes from, since it is nowhere taught in the Bible. The Bible teaches the exact opposite. It does not matter if you are in the church service. It does not matter if you claim to know God and waive your Christian blanket all around town. God showed us how He feels about this kind of hollow mentality when He exposed the hearts of the Israelites.

These people draw near with their mouths and honor Me with their lips, but have removed their hearts far from Me, and their fear toward Me is taught by the commandment of men. (Isaiah 29:13)

So where does this mindset come from? How does a person develop the idea that he can simply attend church to avoid an eternity in hell? I do not believe we have to look far for the answer to this question. All we need is a mirror. Take a look and tell me what you see—flesh. This distorted mindset is deeply rooted in our sin nature. Paul says in Romans 8,

> For those who live according to the flesh set their minds on the things of the flesh, but those who live according to the Spirit, the things of the Spirit. For to be carnally minded is death, but to be spiritually minded is life and peace. Because the carnal mind is enmity against God; for it is not subject to the law of God, nor indeed can be. So then, those who are in the flesh cannot please God. (Romans 8:5–8)

If individuals are living for themselves and worldly things throughout the week, they are also thinking selfishly about the eternal life that they desire to attain. Like me, they want the quick fix—the easy way out. Religion is the answer then. They will hide their worldliness with the Christian blanket they obtained when they "accepted" Christ by saying the "special" prayer, walking the aisle that one Sunday morning, or sitting on the side of their bed as their mom led them in prayer. But this is not the true Christian walk. This is a religion constructed by fleshly minds only interested in doing the bare minimum of what they *think* will get them to heaven. In his book *Man—The Dwelling Place of God*, A. W. Tozer said,

> A whole new generation of Christians has come up believing that it is possible to "accept" Christ without forsaking the world.[2]

According to Jesus, this is anything but a new kind of problem. Jesus tells a man in Luke 13 that there will be many who have this attitude.

> And He went through the cities and villages, teaching, and journeying toward Jerusalem. Then one said to Him, "Lord, are there few who are saved?" And He said to them, "Strive to enter through the narrow gate, for many, I say to you, will seek to enter and will not be able. When once the Master of the house has risen up and shut the door, and you begin to stand outside and knock at the door, saying, 'Lord, Lord, open for us,' and He will answer and say to you, 'I do not know you, where you are from,' then you will begin to say, 'We ate and drank in Your presence, and You taught in our streets.' But He will say, 'I tell you I do not know you, where you are from. Depart from Me, all you workers of iniquity.'" (Luke 13:22–27)

---

[2] A.W. Tozer, *Man—The Dwelling Place of God*. (Blacksburg, VA: Wilder Publications, 2009), 48.

Think about this passage for a minute. The people qualified themselves in front of the Master by trying to get Him to remember them. The best that they could come up with was, "We ate and drank in Your presence, and You taught in our streets." How impersonal are these qualifications? "Jesus, we were in the same vicinity. Don't you remember me?"

Jesus, speaking to a Jewish audience, was talking about those Jews who thought they were approved before God simply because they were Jews. Doesn't that sound like the modern-day Christian? Because they claim the name, God will save them. Those described in the parable are prime examples of those who cover themselves with the Christian blanket. Today it just sounds like this: "Look, Jesus…I ate the bread and drank the cup of juice in the church building, and the pastor taught from the pulpit. Don't you remember me? I grew up in the church; I was always in the building. Remember me? I even went to a Christian school! Remember me?"

But what is the Master's response? "I do not know you… depart from Me, all you workers of iniquity." The word used for "workers of iniquity" means evildoers—those who *do* evil. It does not matter if you show up in the building on Sunday. What does your Monday to Saturday look like? What does your life look like? Are you a worker of iniquity? Are you someone who does evil in the sight of a holy God? Are you trying to use the Christian blanket to cover your evil?

> Therefore thus says the Lord God: "Behold, I lay
> in Zion a stone for a foundation, a tried stone,
> a precious cornerstone, a sure foundation;
> whoever believes will not act hastily. Also

I will make justice the measuring line, and righteousness the plummet; the hail will sweep away the refuge of lies, and the waters will overflow the hiding place. Your covenant with death will be annulled, and your agreement with hell will not stand; when the overflowing scourge passes through, then you will be trampled down by it. As often as it goes out it will take you; for morning by morning it will pass over, and by day and by night; it will be a terror just to understand the report." For the bed is too short to stretch out on, and the covering so narrow that one cannot wrap himself in it. (Isaiah 28:16–20)

God says that justice is the measure and righteousness is what has weight. The agreement you have made with death, saying in effect, "I call myself a Christian, so I am going to heaven," will not stand. Anything short of the righteousness of God's precious Cornerstone will collapse like the house of the fool who built on the sand (Matthew 7:24–27).

Try as we might to cover ourselves with the lies of our fabricated Christian blanket, the Bible says we will be exposed in the end—unable to wrap ourselves in it. When we finally come face to face with a perfectly just and righteous God, there is nothing we can do to hide our true actions, intentions, thoughts, and feelings. And on that day, many will find that their Christian blanket is useless in His presence.

INTER-ACTUAL EXERCISE:

1. Can you think of a time when you believed you were safe from spiritual condemnation because you claimed to be a Christian or attended church regularly?
2. How did you justify your conclusion? Was it based on fact? Or did your flesh convince you that you were "covered?"
3. Do some self-evaluating.
    a. Do you call yourself a Christian? What does that mean to you?
    b. Do you attend church regularly? If so, is your heart in it? Or do you go because of an obligation?
    c. Do you read the Bible regularly?
    d. What do your thoughts and behaviors look like during the week?
4. If you lived in a place like China or Turkey, would you still be committed to following Jesus? Why or why not?
5. If Jesus asked you why He should let you in to be with Him, what reasons would you give to convince Him?

CHAPTER 2

THE GOOD WORKS BLANKET

For they being ignorant of God's righteousness,
and seeking to establish their own righteousness,
have not submitted to the righteousness of God.
—Romans 10:3

I have heard people say, "I chose Christianity as my religion, but my kids can choose whatever they like," as if Christianity was just a way of life (hence "religion") and that whatever someone "likes" determines what is true. Granted, people can and do *choose* what they believe but that does not make it true. People will say, "Truth is relative, and this is *my* truth." The fact is that they believe anyone can cover themselves with whatever blanket makes them *feel* good. Similar to how my blanket could not keep me from harm as a child, these blankets of religion are not going to do anything to protect us when we stand before God to give an account of our lives.

The "good works blanket" is different from the Christian blanket. The Christian blanket claims the name but does nothing to back it up; the good works blanket is a covering of good works that a person uses for protection from judgment after death. It is used for justification by those who are willing to put the work in to creating and maintaining it.

Two distinct types of people use the good works blanket. The first is someone who thinks that he is generally a "pretty good person" and that his good works will outweigh the bad in the end. The person thinks, "God is a good guy and does not send good people to hell, right?" The second is a person who is stuck on the belief that he is in good standing with God based solely on the works he performs. In other words, this person has grown up in the church, has head knowledge of God, and knows that Jesus paid for his sins. The only motivation for doing the right things is that the person knows that it is what he is *supposed* to do. This individual is not doing it out of love for the Savior.

GOOD WORKS—JESUS WHO?

The first group of people who use the good works blanket give little thought to who God is and may not even know the Gospel. They believe that there *is* a God or a "higher power," and that if they simply treat everyone well, then everything will turn out fine. They do not think of themselves as sinners; that term is reserved for the Hitlers and Stalins of the world. Some in this group may even think that "all roads lead to heaven." While the good works blanket may cover their ignorance with blissful thinking, it also blinds their eyes to the truth.

The Bible teaches that no living being can do enough good works to earn a ticket to heaven. There is no good deed that could ever satisfy the righteous judgment of God. At the end of the day, we are all sinners hopelessly in need of a savior. Scripture says, "All have sinned and fallen short of the glory of God" and "the wages of sin is death" (Romans 3:23, 6:23). Even *if* your good works are more numerous than the bad, James says, "For whoever keeps the whole law and yet stumbles at just one point is guilty of breaking all of it" (James 2:10). In other words, even if you are *mostly* good, you are still guilty of breaking the law of God.

In Isaiah 59, God describes the people of that day (who are no different than the people of today) saying,

> No one calls for justice, nor does any plead for truth. They trust in empty words and speak lies; they conceive evil and bring forth iniquity. They hatch vipers' eggs and weave the spider's web; he who eats of their eggs dies, and from that which is crushed a viper breaks out. Their webs will not become garments, nor will they cover themselves with their works; their works are works of iniquity, and the act of violence is in their hands. (Isaiah 59:4–6)

No one searches for truth. Instead, our natural tendency is to believe what we like, and many people trust that, since they are "good people," they will be able to cover themselves with their blankets of good works. But God says that "their webs *will not* become garments, nor will they cover themselves with their works" (emphasis added). It is impossible for our works to cover our trespasses.

Someone might say, "So God sends people to hell just

because they do not believe in Him? That seems arrogant and selfish! Why would I want to believe in a God like that anyway?" But what that person fails to understand is that God is perfect in *all* His attributes, not just the ones that *we* want or like. Because we have broken the moral law established by God, it is not God who is sending us to hell. It is the natural consequence of breaking the law (Romans 3:19–20, 6:23), as the natural consequence of letting go of a rock is the rock falling to the ground. In other words, no one would think it arrogant and selfish for a judge to sentence to prison someone who has committed a crime. We would consider the judge *just* and *fair* because he is enforcing the law in the form of a penalty for the lawbreaker's actions—that is, the natural consequence of breaking the law.

The problem is that "every way of a man is right in his own eyes," thus setting up his own standards to live by and ignoring natural consequences of moral wrongdoing (Proverbs 21:2). Relative truth has become an all-too-common theme in America today when it comes to spiritual and moral matters. Yet no one would think of imparting such a theory to a supreme court judge after being found guilty of a high crime. Even if someone were to make such a statement, it would not absolve him from guilt or free him from the given sentence.

> Every way of a man is right in his own eyes, But the Lord weighs the hearts. (Proverbs 21:2)

According to the Bible, the God of the universe is perfectly just (Deuteronomy 32:4). Therefore, the law that He has established must be followed. Perfect justice requires a penalty to be bestowed for any law that is broken. According to the Bible, *that* penalty, for the breaking of God's law, is death (Romans 6:23).

You might say, "How could God do that? Couldn't He be merciful and gracious and let people off the hook?" Actually... yes! But remember, God is perfect in *all* His attributes. There was only one way in which God could "let us off the hook" while remaining perfect in justice, and it involves His perfect love. For God to remain perfect in justice and for us *not* to receive the penalty for breaking the law, someone without fault had to receive the penalty on our behalf. God killed His own Son because of the law that *we* had broken, satisfying God's need for perfect justice. Those who will genuinely believe and put their faith in this Jesus will not only be saved from the penalty of their sin, they will also be changed forever through the indwelling of the Holy Spirit and will spend eternity *with* Him (2 Corinthians 5:17; Romans 8:11; John 14:3). That is not selfish arrogance—that is perfect justice satisfied by outrageous love. As the old hymn goes,

> Because the sinless Savior died
> My sinful soul is counted free
> For God the just is satisfied
> To look on Him and pardon me
> To look on Him and pardon me.[3]

---

[3] Charitie Lees Bancroft, "Before the Throne of God Above," Hymnary.org, accessed February 20, 2022, https://hymnary.org/text/before_the_throne_of_god_above_i_have_a_.

GOOD WORKS—THE ENDLESS LOOP

The second group who use the good works blanket have gone to church their whole lives, speak the "Christianese" language, and play the part. They grew up learning about how serving in the church is what Christians are *supposed to do*. While that may be true, these people hold onto good works and service, never really grabbing onto Jesus Himself. Instead, they are trapped in an endless loop of confusion, running around doing all the things that a good Christian is *supposed to do*, but never slowing down long enough to assess their hearts or have an encounter with Jesus. I call these people "Make-Believers" (a term I adopted from J. Vernon McGee)—and I was one of them.

A Make-Believer is lost in the church. This person claims to know who he is but some part of him feels lost and alone in a church where people do not always share their struggles. Not that other people do not *have* struggles, but they are most often reluctant to reveal them in the church setting. Therefore, to the Make-Believer, they appear to have their lives together. This causes the Make-Believer to feel alone in his sorrow and disconnected from everyone else in the church. The person knows that Jesus is the answer and desperately tries to give his life over to Him, but finds himself pondering what that *really* means.

For many, this desperation simply leads them to give progressively more of their time and talents to the church and to ministry because they are told to "just keep pressing on." This motivates the knitting process of the good works blanket. From here, it grows bigger and bigger until the Make-Believer is left completely wrapped up in feelings of confusion and burden.

The Make-Believer struggles to read his Bible regularly and rarely prays except for before meals and before communion, believing there will be consequences if he does not. The person seldom volunteers to pray in a group, or always does. However, if he prays in a group, he prays fancy words and tries to say the right things or catchy phrases he has heard others use in order to sound spiritual.

I remember a specific time when I was young, and my grandmother opened her prayer with "Dear heavenly Father" instead of what I always had said, which was "Dear Jesus." What Grandma said was much more sophisticated and grown-up, so I started to open my prayers praying to my heavenly Father— though I could not comprehend all that it meant. Please do not misunderstand me; Jesus praised childlike faith, but that is not what I am addressing. Rather, I am addressing the issue of someone who is playing the part, saying the words, and doing the actions, but never meaning them with the heart.

> Orthodoxy, or right opinion, is, at best, a very slender part of religion. Though right tempers cannot subsist without right opinions, yet right opinions may subsist without right tempers. There may be a right opinion of God without either love or one right temper toward Him. Satan is proof of this. [4]

Those who are in this place, or have been here before, know exactly what I am speaking of. A Make-Believer thinks that

---

[4] A.W. Tozer, *The Pursuit of God: The Human Thirst for the Divine* (Chicago, IL: Moody Publishers, 2015), 4.

he is saved but will most likely come to a crossroads driven by frustration with the way things currently are. He may even become so overwhelmed with questions that he gives up and throws away the good works blanket, trading it in for the Christian blanket (discussed in the last chapter), or discarding the name of Christ altogether.

This was my story after so many years of digging my heels into serving in the church. I became so tired of the same old meaningless serving I did all the time. I found myself always too tired or too busy for reading the Bible and praying, yet I plunged myself deeper into serving, thinking that would make me *feel* better and *feel* secure in my salvation like everyone else around me. However, it only caused the questions inside my head to become louder.

Now, I want to be clear that questioning, and even sometimes feeling "lost in church" or unsure of your relationship with Christ, does not mean that you are *not* a true child of God. Questions are healthy and feeling lost is usually a tool used by the Holy Spirit to bring the Christian back to his knees, and back to Jesus. In fact, God calls Israel to reason with Him (Isaiah 1:18). If you pay attention as you read the biblical accounts, you will notice that most of those whose hearts were set on God experienced doubts, questions, fears, and trials often. Think of the psalmist, John the Baptist, the apostle Peter, and others. I will cover these challenges of the Christian faith more in the last chapter of the book. However, if you cannot recall a time when you were *actually* in love with the person of Jesus and find yourself asking what that means, then maybe you need to examine your heart and evaluate whether you are in the faith. Paul instructs the church in Corinth, saying,

> Examine yourselves as to whether you are in the faith. Test yourselves. Do you not know yourselves, that Jesus Christ is in you?—unless indeed you are disqualified. But I trust that you will know that we are not disqualified. (2 Corinthians 13:5–6)

Paul says that the one who has put his faith in Jesus Christ knows that he is a child of God, for by the Spirit His children cry out, "Abba, Father" (Romans 8:15–17). The Make-Believer, though he may never admit it to you or even to himself, has a large amount of insecurity welling up inside of his heart. As the person's good works blanket grows in size, so does his insecurity. The person always needs to add more good works to the blanket in order to *merit* his salvation. This is more commonly known as legalism. The Make-Believer seeks to alleviate his insecurity by simply increasing activity rather than coming to the feet of the Savior for the grace that is freely given.

In Matthew 7, Jesus states that there will be people who call Him "Lord," but who do not live as though He is Lord of their lives. They do not do the will of the Father but instead, they practice lawlessness. Does this not sound like the good works blanket?

> "Not everyone who says to Me, 'Lord, Lord,' shall enter the kingdom of heaven, but he who does the will of My Father in heaven. Many will say to Me in that day, 'Lord, Lord, have we not prophesied in Your name, cast out demons in Your name, and done many wonders in Your

name?' And then I will declare to them, 'I never knew you; depart from Me, you who practice lawlessness!'" (Matthew 7:21–23)

The people in this passage say that they prophesied, cast out demons, and did many wonders in the name of Jesus, but not one of them did Jesus know. A person does not "enter the kingdom of heaven" by works—even works of *power* in the name of Jesus.

INTER-ACTUAL EXERCISE:

1. Have you ever thought you could get to heaven by doing enough good to outweigh the bad? Did you ever feel like you succeeded?

2. What is your reaction to the statement that Christ does not, in fact, require you to do any good works in order to be saved and go to heaven? What *does* He require of you?

3. Have you ever viewed Christianity as just another way someone may or may not choose to live instead of *the true way* to eternal life?

4. Can you relate to the mindset and desperation of the Make-Believer? How can someone be freed from this endless loop of confusion?

CHAPTER 3

NO MORE BLANKETS

Therefore lay aside all filthiness and overflow
of wickedness, and receive with meekness the
implanted word, which is able to save your souls.

—James 1:21

Have you ever played truth or dare? Let me explain how
it goes. One person starts and gives another person the
option of choosing between truth or dare. If the second person
chooses truth, the other person then poses a question, and
the second person must answer honestly and truthfully. If he
chooses dare, then he must complete whatever dare is given.
Now, imagine you are playing this game, you choose truth,
and the person asks you what your deepest, darkest secret is.
You would probably uncover something that *is* a secret but
turns out to be funny for the sake of the game—rather than
laying the most vulnerable and insecure part of your life out
for everyone to see.

How we handle the truth part of this game can resemble
what we do throughout our lives. We might occasionally come

clean to ourselves about some aspects of the skeleton in the closet, but we try to keep the secrets that are deepest and darkest (and often most painful) as hidden as possible. In the past, I worked hard to bury a few secrets of mine particularly deep so that I would forget they existed. I am willing to guess that most people, if not all, have done the same. Such secrets are made up of the worst things about us, locked away in a lead box, and thrown down a hole, never to be seen again—by us or anyone else.

This deep darkness in our souls is one of the major reasons that we seek to cover ourselves with the blankets of religion. We *know* that there is something wrong inside of us and we try desperately to cover our shame and our guilt. We may think we have succeeded in destroying or covering these secrets and ridding our lives of them, but there is One who knows about them and always has.

God knew about our secrets before they ever even *became* secrets. Why then do we indulge our human nature and try to hide from Him? We hide from Him (as if it were possible) "among the trees of the garden" (Genesis 3:8). We are covered in our blankets; we have sewn fig leaves together for our coverings—but no more.

SINCE THE FALL

The Bible tells us that there is nothing new under the sun (Ecclesiastes 1:9), and this is definitely true regarding our desire to hide our sin and shame from God. The first sin ever committed was followed by hiding from God (Genesis 3). The profound response of God in this instance though, was to call to the man, "Where are you?" (Genesis 3:8). This is profound because we know that God, in His omniscience, was fully aware of where the man was physically and spiritually. But the man, even in his newfound knowledge of good and evil, had become lost within himself, having rejected God's command and having been found naked before Him. God exposes Adam's shame and separation from Him by asking, "Where are you?"

The reality is that God knows all things and He always has. This has huge implications for everyone, believers and nonbelievers. God knows every intimate detail about you, from the color of your underwear to the number of hairs on your head; from what you thought about two years ago to the sin you indulged in yesterday behind closed doors. God cannot learn. He knew from eternity past all that has happened, all that is, and all that will happen in the future. He knew that Adam and Eve would choose to reject Him. And he knew that you and I would reject him also.

> For the word of God is alive and active. Sharper than any double-edged sword, it penetrates even to dividing soul and spirit, joints and marrow; it judges the thoughts and attitudes of the heart. Nothing in all creation is hidden from God's sight. Everything is uncovered and laid bare before the eyes of him to whom we must give account. (Hebrews 4:12–13 NIV)

The words used in Greek for *uncovered* and *laid bare* are terms that convey nakedness. This graphic picture is exactly how we are viewed in God's sight, and it is His Word that cuts into us to expose this reality in our hearts. No blanket can protect from this sharp instrument of God. It cuts fast and it cuts deep. God uses it to reveal what is in our hearts and expose that which must be disposed of. There is nothing hidden (Psalm 44:21, 139:4).

> The heart is deceitful above all things, and desperately wicked; who can know it? I, the Lord, search the heart, I test the mind, even to give every man according to his ways, according to the fruit of his doings. (Jeremiah 17:9–10)

THE FACTUAL EXPOSED

At the beginning of Luke 10, Jesus appoints seventy disciples and sends them out to spread the Gospel, "Two by two ahead of him to every town and place where He was about to go." He gives them instructions not to take anything with them but to go into the towns and stay with the people there. If the people would not accept them, they were to have nothing to do with the town; they were to shake the dust off their feet and move on to the next town. These seventy disciples were Jesus's workers sent "into His harvest field." He gave them supernatural power and sent them out to perform signs and wonders amongst the people in the towns they visited. When they returned, they were exceedingly thrilled about the things that had occurred.

> Then the seventy returned with joy, saying, "Lord, even the demons are subject to us in Your name." And He said to them, "I saw

Satan fall like lightning from heaven. Behold, I give you the authority to trample on serpents and scorpions, and over all the power of the enemy, and nothing shall by any means hurt you. Nevertheless, do not rejoice in this, that the spirits are subject to you, but rather rejoice because your names are written in heaven." (Luke 10:17–20)

Wait a minute! Wait a minute! Jesus, You are telling me that we should not rejoice over Pastor So-and-So's spiritual gifts? You are telling me that we should not rejoice over the unbelievable supernatural power and authority that tramples Satan?

Jesus tells His disciples that their focus is misplaced. It is not about the good deeds they do or even the power that He had given them to carry out His work (even though their ministry was successful in kicking Satan in the teeth, so to speak). Rather, what mattered most was that they had been saved by the grace of an almighty God and their names were written in heaven. In other words, Jesus reminds them that their salvation had nothing to do with anything *they* had done. They deserved eternal punishment, just like those He had sent them to. Yet God, because of His great love, extended His grace through Jesus alone; the power that He had given them was to be used in humility and recognition of that fact to reach the rest of humanity and spread the impact of this great message.

Have you ever considered the fact that Satan was originally given his power from God? His downfall was that he took pride in the power and authority that had been *given* to him.

He abused what was meant to be a blessing and he became obsessed with the idea of becoming a god himself. If we are not careful, we could fall into the same prideful trap that leads to rejection (Isaiah 14:12–15).

Today, however, as unfortunate as it may be, many do fall into this trap. We have pastors all across the globe who teach only what the people want to hear and abuse the position of authority that God has given them. They contradict the Bible and teach a gospel that God wants you to be "healthy, wealthy, and wise." Therefore, do whatever you need to do to make yourself feel good, obtain possessions, increase your knowledge, and God will be pleased and save you. But this is far from the truth.

> Let no one deceive himself. If anyone among you seems to be wise in this age, let him become a fool that he may become wise. For the wisdom of this world is foolishness with God. For it is written, "He catches the wise in their own craftiness"; and again, "The Lord knows the thoughts of the wise, that they are futile." (1 Corinthians 3:18–20)

THE GREATEST LOVE AFFAIR

I recently attended a funeral where the pastor performing the service seemed very impersonal in a way that almost ruined the somberness of the ceremony. But the worst part was that he quoted Scripture out of context and made it sound as though it does not matter what the person inside the casket believed;

Jesus saved him, and he is going to heaven. In contrast, the daughter of the man who had passed away got up to speak and explained the truth of God's Word, which she knew the people in attendance sorely needed to hear. Jesus *did* die for everyone, but they *must* repent of their sins, acknowledge Him as Lord, and surrender their lives to Him. Otherwise, they are destined for an eternity of separation from God in hell (Acts 4:12, John 5:24–30, Revelation 20:15).

Everyone who spoke at the funeral commented on how many good things the deceased had done in his life. However, his daughter explained with clarity that it was *not* because of anything he had done that she would see him again in heaven. It did not matter that he was a wonderful husband, father, and grandfather. It did not matter that he was a firefighter and had saved dozens of lives during his time in the service. What mattered was that he put his faith and trust in the Lord Jesus Christ before he died.

In Matthew 19, Jesus encounters a man who comes running and kneels before Him. Three of the gospels record this encounter, and we can conclude that this man was young, wealthy, and had a position of authority—everything anyone could want in this world, right? (We as humans all want to have enough money so that we do not have to worry about income. We can just live our lives spending and doing anything we want. And the younger we get the money, the more time we have on earth to live using it). The young man asks Jesus, "What good thing shall I do that I may have eternal life?" In His response, Jesus masterfully implies that if the man wanted to "*do*" something, then he needed to follow the law. The man replies, "All these I have kept, what do I still lack?" Jesus tells him to sell all his possessions, give to the poor, take up his cross, and follow Him. But the man went away, unwilling to give up his possessions, and unwilling to surrender himself to Jesus.

It is our desire to work our way to heaven that confuses us into thinking that a blanket covering will suffice. But the truth is that we are missing the same thing that the rich young ruler was missing. He valued his possessions, wealth, and position of authority more than Jesus. He wanted to add eternity to his wealth but did not want to give up his world to follow Jesus, not realizing that Jesus is better than earthly possessions. Jesus also exposed a similar mentality in the Pharisees in John 5 when He said,

> "And the Father Himself, who sent Me, has testified of Me. You have neither heard His voice at any time, nor seen His form. But you do not have His word abiding in you, because whom He sent, Him you do not believe. You search the Scriptures, for in them you think you have eternal life; and these are they which testify of Me. But you are not willing to come to Me that you may have life." (John 5:37–40)

The Scriptures that Jesus is referring to are the Old Testament Scriptures consisting of the law of Moses, the poetic books, and the prophetic books. The Scriptures had declared that there would be a New Covenant of permanent deliverance from sin through the coming Messiah (Jeremiah 31:31–34, Psalm 53). But the Pharisees wanted to continue doing the works of the law, relying on their *own* righteousness, rather than coming to Jesus for salvation from sin. Coming to Jesus for rescue would mean that they recognized they were completely unable to cover their sin with their self-righteousness. Coming to Jesus for rescue would mean that they would be denying their pride by accepting the love of God. As verse forty-two says, "But I know you, that you do not have the love of God in you." The Pharisees loved themselves and wanted to work their *own* way to heaven, just like the rich young ruler. They wanted to cover themselves with their own blankets and in so doing rejected the love of God and the life that is in Jesus Himself.

So, what am I saying? It is important, if not imperative, for us to understand the love that God has for us and just how much He has done. There is absolutely nothing that we can do to merit God's favor. There is absolutely nothing we can do to cover our sin which spits in the face of God. There is nothing we can do to impress God. We are fallen and evil, every single one of us. The knowledge of our inability to get to God and of our sin against Him should break our hearts to a point of surrender that leads to the greatest love affair there has ever been.

That is what all of history points to, hinges on, clings to— God's love being displayed by sending His Only Son, Jesus, to die on our behalf. Our behalf! We who spit in His face with our sin, the ones who constantly reject His love and mercy to try to attain for ourselves the desires of our hearts.

God did not give everything He had for us just so that He could "let us off the hook." No—He did it to show His great and awesome love, that those who would be humbled by His gift of grace would never stop loving Him in return. "We love

Him because He first loved us" (1 John 4:19). Without God first loving us, we would not even be capable of loving Him.

> You see, at just the right time, when we were still powerless, Christ died for the ungodly. Very rarely will anyone die for a righteous person, though for a good person someone might possibly dare to die. But God demonstrates his own love for us in this: While we were still sinners, Christ died for us. (Romans 5:6–8)

He chose the greatest display of love and laid Himself down for us sinners so that He could have an intimate relationship with us, not so that He could simply pardon people from eternal punishment. You see, heaven would be hell if Jesus were not there—let me repeat that—heaven would be hell if Jesus were not there. Without Him, eternity would not be worth living. That is why Scripture says, "The gift of God is eternal life *in Christ Jesus our Lord*" (Romans 6:23; emphasis added). And again, "Now this is eternal life: that they know you, the only true God, and Jesus Christ, whom you have sent" (John 17:3).

Jesus poured out His blood on our behalf, removing the sin that separated us from God so that we could be brought to God (1 Peter 3:18). And in this substitutionary sacrifice, His love would be displayed, and we would desire to enter an everlasting relationship of love with Him (Romans 5:6–11).

God does not call us to do charitable deeds to receive salvation, nor does He call us to simply say "I believe in Jesus" and yet live however we want. He calls us to give up and put our faith in *Him*. He calls us to recognize our depravity and realize how truly unworthy we are to be loved by the almighty God—to rejoice that we, who are His, have been blessed with such a privilege that our names have been written in heaven.

No more blankets. Instead, we have put on Christ as our covering and now have a cross to carry (Galatians 3:27, Luke 9:23).

INTER-ACTUAL EXERCISE:

1. How does it make you feel knowing that nothing in your life is hidden from God? Read Hebrews 4:13 and Psalm 139. How will the truths of these Scriptures affect the way you communicate with God on a daily basis?

2. The Bible says that all humans are born sinful and in need of saving. Do you believe this truth? Write down one or two references where the Bible explains the origin of our sin nature.

3. Explain the significance of this statement: "No more blankets. Instead, we have put on Christ as our covering and now have a cross to carry." Read Luke 9:23–26.

4. Are you ready to throw off the useless blankets of "Christianity" and good works and commit to following Christ in a real way? Take some time to pray and ask God to examine your heart concerning this area in your life (Psalm 139:23–24).

CHAPTER 4

SHOW ME YOUR FAITH

> Though you have not seen Him, you love Him.
> Though you do not now see Him, you believe
> in Him and rejoice with joy that is inexpressible
> and filled with glory, obtaining the outcome of
> your faith, the salvation of your souls.
>
> —1 Peter 1:8–9 ESV

I hope that by this point you have realized there is a drastic difference between intellectual acknowledgment and genuine faith. This difference, however, is not always visible from the outside since those playing the part play it well.

Jesus explains this outward similarity in Matthew 13 when He speaks the parable of the wheat and the tares (Matthew 13:24–30). In the parable, Jesus explains that when first planted, the wheat and the tares are difficult to tell apart. However, once both plants have matured, *then* the distinct characteristics will be visible for the harvest. The same is true for the *factual* and *actual* Christians.

Where then does the root of this difference lie? In the heart.

Choosing to put your faith in Jesus and surrender your will is not an intellectual determination—it is a decision of the heart. To illustrate this contrast even further, I would like to draw your attention to a man by the name of Charles Blondin.

Can you imagine a tightrope stretched over a quarter of a mile and spanning the breadth of Niagara Falls? The thundering sound of the pounding water drowning out all other sounds as you watch a man step onto the rope and walk across! This stunning feat made Charles Blondin famous in the summer of 1859. He walked 160 feet above the falls several times back and forth between Canada and the United States as huge crowds on both sides looked on with shock and awe. Once he crossed in a sack, once on stilts, another time on a bicycle, and once he even carried a stove and cooked an omelet! On July 15, Blondin walked backward across the tightrope to Canada and returned pushing a wheelbarrow. The story is told that it was after pushing a wheelbarrow across while blindfolded that Blondin asked for some audience participation. The crowds had watched and "Ooooohed" and "Aaaaahed!" He had proven that he could do it; of that, there was no doubt. It is said that he asked his audience, "Do you believe I can carry a person across in this wheelbarrow?" Of course, the crowd shouted that yes, they believed! It was then that

Blondin posed the question, "Who will get in
the wheelbarrow?"[5]

The story of Charles Blondin provides us with a perfect
example of the difference between faith and intellectual
acknowledgment. The entire crowd *acknowledged* that Blondin
could wheelbarrow a person across the tightrope, but when it
came time for someone to put action to their acknowledgment,
no one would get into the wheelbarrow. *Faith* in Blondin
would have resulted in someone getting into the wheelbarrow,
trusting that he would safely wheel them across the Falls. Such
faith was displayed by Blondin's manager a few months later
when he rode on Blondin's back across the Falls.

One of the most clear and concise biblical examples of this
is found in James 2:14–26. If you look carefully at this passage,
you will see both intellectual acknowledgment *and* genuine
faith. James declares that even demons believe. However, this
does not make them redeemed beings. Even though they know
of God and believe in His *existence*, they reject Him as their
Lord and will be separated from Him in judgment forever.
Demons are a biblical example of what befalls those who have
intellectual acknowledgment *without* genuine faith. Faith
involves the freewill choice to totally surrender our lives and
submit to the Lordship of Christ, and this surrender is made
evident by fruit or actions.

---

5   Susan Smart, "Charles Blondin Story—Faith on a Tightrope," CreativeBibleStudy.
com, accessed February 21, 2022, https://www.creativeBiblestudy.com/Blondin-
story.html.

But someone will say, "You have faith, and I have works." Show me your faith without your works, and I will show you my faith by my works. (James 2:18)

What I am saying, and what the Bible is saying, is that there is an enormous difference between acknowledgment in the mind and faith in the heart. Every individual must have a personal encounter with Jesus Christ Himself and come to know in his heart that "this is indeed the Christ," resulting in full and total surrender to Him.

> But what does it say? "The word is near you, in your mouth and in your heart" (that is, the word of faith which we preach): that if you confess with your mouth the Lord Jesus and believe in your heart that God has raised Him from the dead, you will be saved. For with the heart one believes unto righteousness, and with the mouth confession is made unto salvation. For the Scripture says, "Whoever believes on Him will not be put to shame." For there is no distinction between Jew and Greek, for the same Lord over all is rich to all who call upon Him. For "whoever calls on the name of the Lord shall be saved. (Romans 10:8–13)

THE FRUIT OF LOVE

> Thus in all our prayers we must request God's grace, with a humble resolution to do our duty, else we mock God, and show that we do not rightly value the mercies we pray for.[6]
>
> —Matthew Henry

It may seem confusing that the next natural step following salvation is fruit or good works. But wait, did I not just prove in the previous chapters that it is not good works that save a person? As we have seen in Scripture, it *is* possible to do good works and not love God. Yet, if you love God, you *will* do good works.

For instance, you can hate your job and yet still work extremely hard at it because of the reward that you get at the end of the week: your paycheck. However, just because you work hard does not mean that you love your job; it simply shows that you want the reward. Conversely, if you love your job, you will work hard at it, not for the reward, but for the sake of the love that you have for the work itself. It is the same way within the Christian community. Some are working hard to receive heaven as their reward, while others are working because they love the Savior, and the joy of heaven for them is that they will be *with* Jesus Himself.

Let me give you another example. Say you are a young man who is deeply in love with a beautiful young woman (or vice

---

6 Matthew Henry, "Matthew Henry's Commentary—Verses 6–9," BibleGateway, accessed July 28, 2022, https://www.biblegateway.com/resources/matthew-henry/Luke.13.6-Luke.13.9.

versa). You are naturally going to do everything you can to show her that you love her. You are going to feed her horses for her; whisk her away to historic sites and gardens; and even run like a goofball across the yard to make her laugh. (Yes, I am speaking of myself—and now she is my wife!) If you genuinely love her, there is nothing you will not do to show her. But the truth of the matter is that you already loved her beforehand. It was not your kindness toward her that brought love into your heart, it was the love in your heart that brought kindness, devotion, and loyalty out.

This is how God desires for our relationship with Him to be. He displayed His love in the most dramatic way possible to get our attention and to save us from our depravity. What should our reaction be? Extraordinary, passionate, "head over heels" love! That love will inevitably show itself through good deeds to please our God and Savior.

> As the Father loved Me, I also have loved you; abide in My love. If you keep My commandments, you will abide in My love, just as I have kept My Father's commandments and abide in His love. (John 15:9–10)

This is the answer to the question, "What does it mean to love God?" that awakened my spirit to the longing in my heart. If our most desperate desire is to remain in the love of Christ, we will, by *His* strength, follow the commands that He has set before us. The more we understand how much God loves us and all He has done for us, the greater our love for Him will become. We will *actually* believe that what He has said is good for us.

IT IS GOD WHO WORKS IN YOU

You may ask, "What if I did love Jesus like that once and my love seems to have faded?" Then I shall direct you to the words of Jesus in His letter to the Church of Ephesus, "Remember therefore from where you have fallen; repent and do the first works" (Revelation 2:5). Love is not a once-done act or feeling toward God (or toward others, for that matter). When God tells His people to love Him with all their heart, soul, and strength, and to love their neighbors as themselves, He is calling them to a lifelong commitment of love (Deuteronomy 6:5, Leviticus 19:18). There will be more on this in the last chapter. As Corrie Ten Boom said,

> Trying to do the Lord's work in your own strength is the most confusing, exhausting, and tedious of all work. But when you are filled with the Holy Spirit, then the ministry of Jesus just flows out of you.[7]

I used to think that I could promise God that I would do better next time. Or, like many others, I would cry out in distress or trouble and say, "God, if you get me out of this, I promise I will..." and you can fill in the blank. Then one

---

[7] Corrie Ten Boom, "Corrie Ten Boom: Quotable Quote," Goodreads, accessed March 4, 2022, https://www.goodreads.com/quotes/51450-trying-to-do-the-lord-s-work-in-your-own-strength.

day I was reading a book, and in it was the statement that we have no power to promise God anything. This simple yet powerful truth hit me between the eyes and resulted in physical prostration before God as I cried out, "God, be merciful to me a sinner!" (Luke 18:13).

With this call to love God, the power to do so is also supplied by God Himself. *He* supplies the power to love Him. *He* supplies the power to obey Him. *He* produces in us, by the Holy Spirit, the fruit that follows genuine faith. Our lives are to be humbly presented to Him in love for the *doing* of His work as we walk in His Spirit (Romans 8:1, 12:1).

> Work out your own salvation with fear and trembling; for it is God who works in you both to will and to do for His good pleasure. (Philippians 2:12–13)

INTER-ACTUAL EXERCISE:

1. What is the difference between doing works to earn salvation (as with the "good works blanket") versus working out your salvation? Read Phil. 2:12–13 and 1 John 2:3–6.
2. Genuine faith begins with love and is displayed through actions. Do you think that your actions reveal that you truly love Jesus?

3. Can you relate to Blondin's story in your own faith journey? Can you think of a time when you had a faith crisis and had to put action to your faith like this? Explain how.

4. God has supplied us with "all things that pertain to life and godliness" (2 Peter 1:3). Are you surrendering to His work *in* you, or are you trying to do the work in your own power?

CHAPTER 5

THE "GODS" OF THE CHRISTIAN

And God said to Moses, "I AM WHO I AM."
And He said, "Thus you shall say to the children
of Israel, 'I AM has sent me to you.'"

—Exodus 3:14

Have you ever listened to music? What am I saying? Of course, you have. Have you ever experienced, when listening to music, an image of the singer you have never seen before forming in your head? Or when you are listening to your favorite radio host, you may picture him or her a certain way, with certain features, hair color, or skin color. Yet, when you *actually* see that person, most of the time he or she looks nothing like what you had pictured. What happened? How did the picture in your head even become what it was?

We often form ideas of who a person is based on what we hear. Once we see the actual picture of the singer or host, or even meet that person face to face, we realize that the ideas we had about his or her identity were wrong. Sometimes, we are even upset that the person did not look at all like how we pictured, wishing we had never seen him or her. We would rather have the individual look like that picture in our head. But now our perception of that person has changed because we know what he or she *actually* looks like.

When I was in high school, I liked a singer named Ed Sheeran. He had a beautiful voice, sang about love, and plucked the guitar strings as if he had been playing since he was born. When I first heard him, I thought he would be what all the girls wanted: handsome, tall, tan, and covered in muscles. He *actually* turned out to be the exact opposite—what a disappointment. I would rather just listen to his music and picture *my* version of what I thought he looked like; it is much better than reality. But the truth is that it does not matter what I picture Ed Sheeran looking like—he is who he is regardless of what I think.

When you think of God, how do you picture Him? (I am sure you knew this is where I was going.) Do you think of the "big man upstairs?" An old man in a chair? The picture of Jesus with long hair and a beard? Pure love? The rule-maker? A combination of all of them? Since "no man has seen God" and there is no real-life portrait of Him that exists, how we picture Him usually forms from a combination of what we have heard about Him from pastors, teachers, parents, and friends.

Frankly, however our picture of God forms in our heads does not matter if it is not true. We can picture God as anything we want, but that does not *make* Him anything we want. I could not magically conjure Ed Sheeran's tall, dark, and handsome features into reality, and we cannot create our own image of the God we want to see. How then do we get a true picture of

God? What *is* the reality? God is who He is, no matter what we *think* or *prefer*. In His own words, "I AM WHO I AM" (Exodus 3:14, John 8:58).

God is constant and never changing. In fact, the Name of God as revealed in the Old Testament—"YHWH"—emphasizes that God is eternal and never changing (Exodus 3:14–15, Malachi 3:6). Therefore, we know that each distinct Person of the Godhead (the Father, Son, and Holy Spirit) is never changing, and we need to make sure that we have the right picture of who each Person of the Trinity is, rather than our distorted image that is based on what we have heard.

THE BEING OF CREATION

Many people who believe that there is a God picture Him as the one who created all things, is all-powerful, and up in the sky somewhere. While He *did* create all things and *is* all-powerful, there is hardly any thought placed on the fact that He is a personal being, even for many Christians. He is just a higher power who can strike you with lightning or bless you with this or that. He is there, He cares, but only when you need Him. I am not saying that He is not these things. He does control all things because He made all things and people recognize this— but that is not *all* He is.

In Acts 17, Paul speaks to a group of Athenian philosophers amid their ruling council, the Areopagus. They all worshiped idols, many idols, yet they still had a sense that there was another god out there that they could not identify. They were afraid that they had missed one and did not want to offend him. Therefore, Paul takes advantage of the opportunity and proclaims to them that this God is the One True God.

> Then Paul stood in the midst of the Areopagus and said, "Men of Athens, I perceive that in all things you are very religious; for as I was passing through and considering the objects of your worship, I even found an altar with this inscription: TO THE UNKNOWN GOD. Therefore, the One whom you worship without knowing, Him I proclaim to you."
> (Acts 17:22–23)

Unfortunately, many Christians live the same way that the Athenian philosophers lived; they worship idols and God just happens to be one of them. They are religious in all they do. They go to church, serve in ministry, and pray before meals, but in their minds and hearts God is still "UNKNOWN" or unknowable. You may say, "Wait, what do you mean? I don't know anyone who still worships idols." People worship all kinds of idols today, from their favorite sports icon or movie star to cars or even knowledge and logic like the Athenians. Many Christians pursue their various idols while at the same time worshiping "THE UNKNOWN GOD." There is little thought to *who* God is, and if He even *can* be known.

Prayers are offered up to Him because—well—He's God. It is what you do when you are in trouble, or you want something. He is treated like a vending machine or a genie in a bottle. Yet, unlike the *I Dream of Jeanie* TV show in the late 1960s, no one wants to know God beyond the bottle, let alone have a relationship with Him that is comparable to marriage.[8] However, this is the exact kind of intimate relationship that God wants to have with us. To be clear, God is *not* a genie or a vending machine but rather a loving husband.

God the Father describes Himself as a husband to Israel in the Old Testament many times. In the New Testament, Jesus is described as the husband of the Church. That would include all those who have put their faith and trust in Jesus (Isaiah 54:5 and 62:5; Jeremiah 2:2 and 32, 3:14 and 20, and 31:32; Hosea 2:16; Matthew 9:15; 2 Corinthians 11:2; Ephesians 5:23; Revelation 19:7 and 21:9). Why then, do we often speak to Him as if our words must travel millions of miles before they reach Him? Our conversation with Him is sometimes short, dull, insincere—and many times—simply words said with our eyes closed. Do we think that God is so distant that we cannot connect with Him? Is He so distant that we cannot *know* Him? Is He simply the Being that created the universe? Who is God?

OTHER VERSIONS OF THE CHRISTIAN "GOD"

The Understanding God of the Christian accepts any and all excuses for the sins you have committed. He *understands* that your six-year-old's baseball game is more important than attending church on Sunday. He *understands* if the physical relationship between two people goes too far because—well— they are getting married in a few months anyway. He seems to

---

[8] For those of you not familiar with the TV show, it was an American sitcom that aired from 1965 to 1970. The show comically depicted a man who found a genie in a bottle. They eventually fell in love and got married.

be very understanding of our "need" to be disobedient because He made us with these desires anyway.

The Forgiving God of the Christian forgives and wipes away all consequences of our sin. For example, have you ever been tempted to sin, and you know it is sin, yet convince yourself that it is okay by telling yourself, "God won't mind this time" or "Jesus will forgive me"? The logic is that Jesus, *as* you are sinning, is forgiving you for the sin you willingly chose to do. How kind of Him. Oh, I almost forgot the best part: there is no consequence for your willful choice of disobedience. What a great God!

The Wrathful God of the Christian is always angry. He wants Christians to beat themselves up over their sin lest they feel His wrath upon them. This God is so angry when we sin that He wants us to wallow in our shame, knowing that we will never get it right. God should just strike us dead. He is unapproachable because of His ever-present wrath. May all beware and be afraid!

The Loving God of the Christian loves—no matter what. Ahhhh…love (sigh). God is just loving and would never punish anyone. He loves and pities all men and women, even if they purposefully sin against Him. There are no consequences, only love. The song, instead, goes something like this, "Jesus loves me this I know, 'cause my pastor tells me so, it don't matter if I sin, He still loves me, so I win!"

The Gracious God of the Christian abounds in grace the more we sin. The Christian continues to sin so that God's grace covers him even more. When I think of this version of God, I think of country songs that talk about God, getting drunk, and hooking up all in the same song. The gracious God of the Christian allows us to do whatever we want, and His grace will still cover us. "Darl'n, God's grace covers all yawl's sin, so let's go get wasted."

In reality, God is not *one* of these—He is all of them, yet *not* in the ways defined above. God is not only understanding and forgiving but also wrathful and hates our sin. He is not only wrathful but loving and gracious. The problem is that we select the attributes of God that we want and make God either too easygoing or exceedingly unapproachable. And to add to this, we distort God by producing earthly concepts of what understanding, forgiveness, wrath, and love are, forgetting that He is the perfection of all of them and by His character, they are defined (not the other way around).

To this day, I and many other believers *still* tend to do this at times. The above descriptions of God's attributes are not accurate. He is perfect in His character. Humanity distorts who He is based on what we have heard, observed, or want; then we wonder why we still do not know the "UNKNOWN GOD." The answer is simple. We do not know God because we keep trying to define Him based on our imagination of what we *think* He is like or what we *want* Him to be like. We are attempting to make God in our image and *that*, the Bible says, is also idolatry (Exodus 20:3–6).

I cannot tell you how many times I have heard the phrase

from my friends, "Well I *think* God…" or "I don't *think* God…" and you can fill in the blank. I have even been guilty of saying this myself. The problem is the same. It does not matter what we *think*—our thoughts about God are only valid if they are in line with Scripture. Scripture is our plumb line, our measuring stick, our map key.

> In my opinion, the greatest sin in the church of Jesus Christ in this generation is ignorance of the Word of God. Many times, I have heard a church officer say, 'Well I don't know much about the Bible, but…' and then he gives his opinion, which often actually contradicts the Word of God! Why doesn't he know much about the Bible? These things were written aforetime for our learning. God wants you to know His Word.[9]

INTER-ACTUAL EXERCISE:

1. Can you think of a time when you were misunderstood by someone because he chose to believe what he *heard* about you instead of going to you to learn the truth? How did that make you feel? Wouldn't you want people to know the real you rather than assume certain

---

[9] J. Vernon McGee, "Romans 9-16," in *Romans* (Nashville, TN: T. Nelson, 1991).

attributes about you, which may or may not even be true? Explain your answer.

2. What are some titles or portrayals of God that you have used when talking about Him throughout your life? How were they incorrect or correct views? Why?

3. Do you ever find yourself saying, "I think God is (fill in the blank)" instead of going to His Word to learn and know the *truth* about Him?

CHAPTER 6

THE GOD OF THE BIBLE

All things have been delivered to Me by My Father, and no one knows the Son except the Father. Nor does anyone know the Father except the Son, and the one to whom the Son wills to reveal Him.

—Matthew 11:27

If we desire to know the one true and real God, then we need to get a picture of who He is that is grounded in truth rather than our whims. How can we do this? Has anyone seen God in order to be able to describe what He is like? Can you or I see God? According to the apostle John, "No one has seen God at any time" (John 1:18, 1 John 4:12). If no one has seen God, then how can He be known?

God's Word, unlike our mental/emotional pictures of God, is always objective and never changing. In 2 Timothy 3:16, Paul tells Timothy that all the Scriptures were inspired, or "breathed out," by God. Therefore, the Bible is our basis of truth that tells us *who* God is from His own breath.

Imagine for a moment that you and your friends are sitting in a room with Jesus, who has appeared in physical form—scars and all. Would it not be ridiculous for you and your friends to start talking about what you *think* Jesus is like when He is sitting in the room and could simply tell you? God has given us the wonderful gift of His Word, through which we can gain a clear picture of who He is. Yet, many who call themselves Christians are reluctant to open His Word to find the concrete truth that can turn their "I *think*" into an "I *know*."

There is another important thing that is necessary to know God intimately through the Bible: you must know His Son, Jesus. In Matthew 11:27, Jesus says, "No one knows the Father except the Son, and the one to whom the Son wills to reveal Him." Therefore, a personal relationship with Jesus Christ is essential to knowing God in an intimate and personal way. Jesus is God in flesh. This is something that I discussed in the earlier chapters of the book.

If we travel back to our discussion of Acts 17, we see that Paul wants to proclaim to the Athenians who this "one whom [they] worship without knowing" is. He says,

> Therefore, the One whom you worship without knowing, Him I proclaim to you: God, who made the world and everything in it, since He is Lord of heaven and earth, does not dwell in temples made with hands. Nor is He worshiped with men's hands, as though He needed anything, since He gives to all life, breath, and all things. And He has made from one blood every nation of men to dwell on all the face of the earth, and

has determined their preappointed times and the boundaries of their dwellings, so that they should seek the Lord, in the hope that they might grope for Him and find Him, though He is not far from each one of us; for in Him we live and move and have our being, as also some of your own poets have said, 'For we are also His offspring.' Therefore, since we are the offspring of God, we ought not to think that the Divine Nature is like gold or silver or stone, something shaped by art and man's devising. Truly, these times of ignorance God overlooked, but now commands all men everywhere to repent, because He has appointed a day on which He will judge the world in righteousness by the Man whom He has ordained. He has given assurance of this to all by raising Him from the dead. (Acts 17:23–31)

Paul describes God as greater than we can even imagine; the Creator of the universe and the sovereign Deity who gives life, breath, movement, being, time, boundaries of geographical living, and all things to His creation every second and every moment of every day forever. You may say, "Isn't this the all-powerful Being in the sky we were just talking about?" Yes! Neither the Bible nor I say that God is *not* the all-powerful Being in the sky—but that He is not *only* the all-powerful Being in the sky. God displays His power through creation, time, and circumstance so that—what does Paul say?—"So that [humankind] should seek the Lord, in the hope that they might grope for Him and find Him." God is not simply looking for us to fear and recognize His incredible and unmistakable power, but wants us to *seek* Him so that we may *find* Him. He wants us to *know* Him and to know that He is an intimate and caring God who desires to be found, loved, and obeyed.

FORGET WHAT YOU THINK YOU KNOW

We often take for granted what we have been told and might even repeat that information as if we were the ones who came up with it. I cannot tell you how many times I have spit out facts about Marvel Universe characters and storylines without having ever read a single comic book myself. I hear a little information here—a little information there—watch a YouTube video—then I talk about the newest Marvel movie as if I am a huge comic book expert and always have been.

The truth is, I hop onto the bandwagon and present the information that I have gathered as if I know the whole picture. I got the information from a secondhand source and, if I am honest, I do not know for sure if the information I have is true. I have been called out before by someone who *does* avidly read the comics. The person corrected me and made it clear that the information I had was wrong. He had gotten his information from the original, true source. Unfortunately, this same thing happens with Christians.

I treated God and His Word this way before I was born again. I was reading the Bible and only making sense of it by what I had heard from teachers and by analogies that were easy for my mind to understand. In other words, I was blindly believing what I had heard and superimposing *that* onto the text as I read the Bible rather than being led by the Spirit to understand the text as it was intended. After being born again, I began to invest substantial amounts of time into studying God's Word and found out that the God I thought I knew was not the God of the Bible. All my ideas of Him that were based on what I had heard over the years were quickly proven wrong.

There were times when I would be engaged in spiritual conversations and would speak about the Bible as if I were an expert. However, at the time, I was speaking from pride, wanting to appear more spiritual than I was. I was not spending time in the Bible or in prayer seeking the Lord. I was gathering my information from here and there and presenting it as if I knew. I took "delight in false humility...vainly puffed up by [my] fleshly mind, and not holding fast to the Head" which is Christ (Colossians 2:18–19). Now looking back, I can see how wrong I was when I could have been right—if I had just opened the book—the Bible.

DO YOU ALSO WANT TO GO AWAY?

Many people in the Christian community have found that their views of God are incorrect when they face struggles in life. As a result, some end up losing faith in God because He did not do what they thought He should. "Losing faith" is a blameless way of saying that they willfully chose to turn away from God. Others, however, choose to seek the Lord in their trouble, that He might expose their inconsistent beliefs and reveal to them the truth.

I fear that many Christians who have grown up in the church will end up like the disciples mentioned in John 6. I have seen it happen to some of my peers and friends. I would have been right there with them had I not chosen to consider the truth behind the troubling questions of my mind. God had placed those nagging thoughts into my head "in the hope that [I] might grope for Him and find Him."

In the latter part of John 6, Jesus introduces the new doctrine of His body being the bread of life saying, "Whoever eats My flesh and drinks My blood has eternal life, and I will raise him up at the last day" (John 6:54). But many of his disciples did not understand Him and so they simply stopped following Him.

> Therefore, many of His disciples, when they heard this, said, "This is a hard saying; who can understand it?" When Jesus knew in Himself that His disciples complained about this, He said to them, "Does this offend you? What then if you should see the Son of Man ascend where He was before? It is the Spirit who gives life; the flesh profits nothing. The words that I speak to you are spirit, and they are life. But there are some of you who do not believe." For Jesus knew from the beginning who they were who did not believe, and who would betray Him. And He said, "Therefore I have said to you that no one can come to Me unless it has been granted to him by My Father." From that time many of His disciples went back and walked with Him no more. (John 6:60–66)

Jesus then turned to His chosen twelve and asked, "Do you

also want to go away?" Peter then responded with words that I am convinced resound in the heart of every true believer.

> "Lord, to whom shall we go? You have the words of eternal life. Also we have come to believe and know that You are the Christ, the Son of the living God." (John 6:68–69)

Will you be like the disciples who stopped following Jesus? Or will you cling to Him, knowing that even though you may not comprehend all He says, He has the words of eternal life, and His words *are* life? Will you choose to forget what you *think* you know, and search the Scriptures to find the truth of who He is?

INTER-ACTUAL EXERCISE:

1. Does the Holy Spirit guide your Bible reading? Or are you reading because it is expected?
2. How can we know the truth about who God is?
3. Take several minutes to list some of the names, titles, and characteristics of God from His Word. Be sure to jot down each reference as you go.
4. God wants us to cling to Him in times of hardship so that we can grow closer to Him and ultimately benefit from the trial. Can you recall times when you went through struggles in your own life? Did those struggles

bring you closer to God? Or did you drift because of them? Explain your answer.

5. Would you react differently in those trials now, after learning what you have about God's true character?

CHAPTER 7

SEEK THE LORD

Oh, give thanks to the Lord! Call upon His name; Make known His deeds among the peoples! Sing to Him, sing psalms to Him; Talk of all His wondrous works! Glory in His holy name; Let the hearts of those rejoice who seek the Lord! Seek the Lord and His strength; Seek His face evermore! Remember His marvelous works which He has done, His wonders, and the judgments of His mouth,

—Psalm 105:1–5

In the Bible, we see that God often commands His people, the Israelites, to *seek* Him that He might be found. A total of forty-three verses throughout Scripture speak of seeking the Lord in some manner. This number does not even include verses like James 4:8 which *imply* seeking the Lord, though the word "seek" is not present ("Draw near to God and He will draw near to you"). In many of these verses, God declares that He will be found by those who seek Him with "all their heart and soul" (Deuteronomy 4:29, 1 Chronicles 22:19, 2 Chronicles 15:12–13).

It seems to me that if we looked at the lives of *most* Christians, we would not describe their actions and their lives as God-seeking. As I explained in chapter five, most people simply look for the kind of God they *want* to see, rather than looking to find out who God has *declared* Himself to be. There is no seeking involved, only naive imagining.

This makes me think of those new thrilling escape rooms. My wife and I went to one a few years ago; it was challenging, fun, and exciting. We were only about ten steps away from escaping the room before our time ran out and the entire world became infected by the zombie virus. In the end, we were unable to solve the clues and discover the cure that would have saved everyone from becoming zombies, but we were satisfied with our score in the game. Can you imagine if we had made it five more steps? Or even two more steps?

The pastor at our church always likes to talk about the sanctification process of born-again believers. He puts forth something like, "You may have ups and downs, but are you ultimately growing closer to God? When we get to heaven, God will complete our sanctification fully, but I don't want Him to have much work left to do." This is his way of expressing that he wants to be open and willing to accept God's work in his life, starting now. He knows that the ultimate perfecting will come in heaven, but he believes we should all strive to get as close as possible to the mark of being like Christ before that time comes. Our desire should be to one day hear our Lord say, "Well done, good and faithful servant" (Matthew 25:21–23). God accomplishes this sanctifying process in our lives all the more abundantly when we earnestly seek Him, desire after Him, and surrender to Him.

Just like in the escape room where my wife and I had to seek for answers to win the game, God desires for us to seek for answers about Himself. Paul uses similar imagery when he exhorts the believers in Corinth to run the race of faith in such a way as to obtain the prize (1 Corinthians 9:24). Through this process, God changes us from the inside out to be the kind of temple that is fit for His home. Someday, our time here on earth will come to an end, just like the time we had to finish the escape room came to an end. The big question is this: when you meet the Lord, how much more work will He have left to do on you to create His perfect temple? Are you running the race to obtain the prize? The Bible emphasizes many times that this earth is not our true home and that we should even hasten or quicken Christ's coming.

> Therefore, since all these things will be dissolved, what manner of persons ought you to be in holy conduct and godliness, looking for and hastening the coming of the day of God, because of which the heavens will be dissolved, being on fire, and the elements will melt with fervent heat? Nevertheless we, according to His promise, look for new heavens and a new earth in which righteousness dwells. (2 Peter 3:11–13)

Did you know that we can hasten His coming? How do we accomplish this? How can we know how to hasten His coming? God has the answer to that question and many more questions concerning the coming of Christ, and He has placed clues in His escape room for us to find. However, many Christians are simply entering the room and sitting down, doing nothing to work toward the end goal. They claim to be seeking the Lord, but they do not have the intent to find Him. What then is seeking without the intent of finding? It is not seeking at all.

In my own life, this was how I behaved growing up. I thought that I was seeking the Lord, but I was simply playing the part. I clearly remember the feeling I would get after spending time at a retreat, conference, or revival service. I would *feel* so incredibly close to God and would *want* to seek Him. I would even read my Bible every day and treat others much nicer in the days following the event. But it never took long for me to feel distant from God once again. I never understood it. I was reading my Bible and praying—why did I not *feel* close to God?

BEYOND THE CHRISTIAN CLICHÉ

One of the big reasons why people walk away from Christ and the Church is that they are seeking a feeling instead of seeking God. They are easily convinced by the world when it tells them that men created the whole of Christianity as just another religion to make people *feel* better. This makes sense to them because they have been chasing after a fleeting feeling their whole lives. If that is why other religions were invented, then how is Christianity any different? They end up abandoning the faith to follow what is right in their own eyes rather than that which is objectively true. I have faced this doubt myself and will discuss it further in the last chapter.

The bottom line is that fellowship with God is *not* simply a feeling, but an intimate interchange, a communion, a closeness, a spiritual intercourse with the living God. It is grounded in truth and confirmed by the testimony of the Holy Spirit (Romans 8:16). This close and constant spiritual interaction with God *will* on occasion result in feelings, good or bad, but is not itself the feeling that is felt. It is much deeper than that.

The best way to illustrate this is with the very intimacy that occurs in marriage. This intimate relation between a husband and a wife, no matter how distorted by the world, was intended by God to give us a vivid picture of the spiritual unity and closeness that occurs with Christ and the Church.

> "For this reason a man shall leave his father and mother and be joined to his wife, and the two shall become one flesh." This is a great mystery, but I speak concerning Christ and the church. (Ephesians 5:31–32)

The word *relationship* is often used within the Christian community to suggest the presence of intimacy with Christ. To me, the word has been all but worn out by those who have once claimed to be in a relationship with Jesus in the past but have since walked away from the faith for one reason or another. How can that be a relationship? Well, I guess you can say that Judas had a relationship with Jesus—but he never experienced the indwelling of the Holy Spirit. Instead, his hard heart continued in secret sin throughout Jesus's three-year ministry, and his life ended with suicide because of his own inner turmoil because of his betrayal (John 12:6, Matthew 27:3–5).

In contrast, the true believer is filled with a longing for God that goes *beyond* the Christian cliché of relationship with God. This is what I am talking about when I say that there is a distinct difference between the *factual* heart and the *actual* heart. A.W. Tozer captured the beating heart of the Spirit-filled believer when he said,

> In this hour of all-but-universal darkness, one cheering gleam appears: Within the fold of conservative Christianity, there are to be found increasing numbers of people whose religious lives are marked by a growing hunger after God Himself. They are eager for spiritual realities and will not be put off with words, nor will they be content with correct "interpretations" of truth. They are thirsty for God, and they will not be satisfied until they have drunk deep at the fountain of living water … The Bible is not an end in itself, but a means to bring men to an intimate and satisfying knowledge of God, that they may enter into Him, that they may delight in His presence, may taste and know the inner sweetness of the very God Himself in the core and center of their being, their spirit. [10]

[10] A.W. Tozer, *The Pursuit of God*, 5.

INTER-ACTUAL EXERCISE:

1. Describe Judas's life and relationship with Jesus. What made his response different than the other disciples?
2. Are you looking forward to the return of Jesus? Read Revelation 21:1–8. What will it be like when believers are reunited with Jesus according to these verses?
3. What is the difference between seeking a feeling about God and seeking God Himself? Is there any way to avoid this deceptive trap?

CHAPTER 8

THE WAR

But you, O man of God, flee these things and pursue righteousness, godliness, faith, love, patience, gentleness. Fight the good fight of faith, lay hold on eternal life, to which you were also called and have confessed the good confession in the presence of many witnesses.

—1 Timothy 6:11–12

Authoring this book has both blessed and challenged me in my faith. At the onset, I felt that God was leading me to share with my peers what I had learned about following Him. Following Jesus involves the forsaking of self and all else. Instead of just adding Him to your life, He becomes your life. All of this I discussed in the earlier chapters. There were times when the words would simply flow onto the page because the Holy Spirit had placed a burden on my heart. Yet, there were other instances when I felt that I could not even think about writing due to confusion and pain, and the book would sit untouched for months.

When I began drafting this book, I did not foresee writing this concluding chapter because at that time I had not yet experienced intense spiritual testing. This chapter was born out of God's testing of my faith. It could be said that the testing of our faith is the next step of the Christian walk. Okay, maybe not the "next step" per se, but it should be our expectation, and we must be prepared.

I have addressed many details of the Christian walk in this book, but it is necessary to close with one aspect that is especially important for us to grasp as we grow in our faith. As believers in Jesus Christ, we are engaged in an all-out war.

WHAT IS THIS WAR?

> This law of sin 'dwells' in us—that is, it adheres as a depraved principle, unto our minds in darkness and vanity, unto our affections in sensuality, unto our wills in a loathing of and aversion from that which is good; and by some, more, or all of these, is continually putting itself upon us, in inclinations, motions, or suggestions to evil, when we would most gladly quit of it. [11]
>
> —John Owen

After I gave my life over to Jesus and surrendered all things to Him, I was taken on an incredible journey of growth for almost a year and a half. I was filled with such boldness in the Spirit and confidence in God's Word and promises. He produced

---

[11] John Owen, *The Nature, Power, Deceit, and Prevalency* (London: Cockerill, 1675), 22.

much fruit through me and allowed me to see many prayers answered. Yet a spirit of doubt began to creep into my life, and I went through a time of depression when I predominantly struggled with the assurance of my salvation. I wondered if I was saved—enough. Have you ever had that thought?

After reading all the previous chapters, you may think that a single thought of doubt destroys all the work that God had done in you previously. That is what I *used* to think. I was afraid that because I had doubts and terrible thoughts it meant that not only was I not saved, but I had betrayed God by questioning the truth at all. I allowed my thoughts and feelings to take the wheel of my faith and be the definer of truth in my life. As a result, I spent many hours in self-inflicted suffering. But this is not what the Bible teaches regarding doubt.

During this period of time, I experienced panic attacks and wondered if God even existed. But how could I think like this? After all that God had done in my life to show Himself to me and to make my salvation sure, how could His existence even be a question in my mind? Of course He exists! I would wonder in those moments if I were to die right then, would I truly be found in Him? Or had my doubt revealed that I never really trusted Him in the first place?

Through these periods of depression and anxiety, I have experienced the reality of spiritual warfare. Our enemy, the devil, hates us and wants more than anything to render us ineffective for God's work. He does this through shame, guilt, doubt, worry, and sin (all things that Jesus destroyed through His death and resurrection). But the enemy keeps bringing it up saying, "Remember this? Do you see what you are doing here? Do you see what you are *not* doing there? God will not forgive you—again." We are, in effect, warring against spiritual powers *and* our own fleshly desires. But the Bible says that Jesus brought an end to the requirements of the law which we could not keep, nailed these things to the cross, and has disarmed the powers that used to hold us captive.

> And you, being dead in your trespasses and the uncircumcision of your flesh, He has made alive together with Him, having forgiven you all trespasses, having wiped out the handwriting of requirements that was against us, which was contrary to us. And He has taken it out of the way, having nailed it to the cross. Having disarmed principalities and powers, He made a public spectacle of them, triumphing over them in it. (Colossians 2:13–15).

Salvation is outside of us, meaning that there is nothing we can do to add to it or even to keep it. We are kept wholly and solely by God Himself (Romans 9:16, Ephesians 1:13, John 10:28–29). God can tell the difference between a person who is saved and struggling through doubts, and a person who is unsaved and playing the part. It may seem like a gray area to us, but to our almighty Father, who is all-knowing, it is black and white. We can rest on the promises of our God and treat the doubts as they are—just the faulting of our human mind.

THE FLESH

As a believer in Jesus Christ, you *will* face war. This is something that Jesus promised, and Paul talked about frequently (John 15:18–21, 2 Corinthians 10:3–6, 1 Timothy 1:18–20, 2 Timothy 2:3–7). It is a warring in your spirit against your flesh and against spiritual forces. In Romans 7, Paul explains the war between the new creation that God had made him, and the old nature that God had put to death and condemned in sinful flesh (Romans 6:2, 8:3, Galatians 2:20, Colossians 2:20). He says,

> For we know that the law is spiritual, but I am of the flesh, sold under sin. For I do not understand my own actions. For I do not do what I want, but I do the very thing I hate. Now if I do what I do not want, I agree with the law, that it is good. So now it is no longer I who do it, but sin that dwells within me. For I know that nothing good dwells in me, that is, in my flesh. For I have the desire to do what is right, but not the ability to carry it out. For I do not do the good I want, but the evil I do not want is what I keep on doing. Now if I do what I do not want, it is no longer I who do it, but sin that dwells within me. So I find it to be a law that when I want to do right, evil lies close at hand. For I delight in the law of God, in my inner being, but I see in my members another law waging war against the law of my mind and making me captive to the

law of sin that dwells in my members. Wretched man that I am! Who will deliver me from this body of death? Thanks be to God through Jesus Christ our Lord! So then, I myself serve the law of God with my mind, but with my flesh I serve the law of sin. (Romans 7:14–25)

There have been many times when I wanted to do what I knew was good, but as Paul says, I did not have the *ability* (in my own strength) to carry it out. Rather, I did the very thing that I hate. Guilt and shame came rushing in and the enemy of my soul pointed at me with a giant finger of condemnation so that I doubted my salvation and felt as though I was dead in my inner being. How could God save me? Does not doing the thing I hate and feeling dead in my spirit prove that I am not in Christ? "Wretched man that I am! Who will deliver me from this body of death? Thanks be to God through Jesus Christ our Lord!" Thanks be to God through Jesus Christ our Lord that the very next verse says,

There is therefore now no condemnation for those who are in Christ Jesus. For the law of the Spirit of life has set you free in Christ Jesus from the law of sin and death. (Romans 8:1–2)

This is the power of salvation in Christ. It is complete and total. It is irrevocable and unbreakable. Christ puts no limit on His forgiveness or measure on our worthiness. *He* is worthy and His righteousness is accounted to us through faith by His grace (Genesis 15:6, Romans 4:5, Ephesians 2:8–9). "So then it depends not on human will or exertion, but on God, who has mercy" (Romans 9:16).

Praise God for His mercy!

THE ENEMY

One of the biggest issues that we have as Christians, and a big reason for why we doubt, is that we forget that there is an actual enemy waging war against us. Just like the serpent in the garden, the enemy is whispering lies to us constantly, enticing us to doubt God and indulge our fleshly thinking. I say to myself, "If I were truly saved, I wouldn't think like that," or "If I really loved Jesus, I wouldn't have sinned like that," or "If the Holy Spirit were *really* inside of me, I wouldn't have *wanted* to sin like that." This is exactly what the enemy wants us to think. He wants us to doubt our eternal security because of the thoughts he encourages us to think. He wants us to question the definitive power of God's promises so that our faith waivers. He wants us to forget, even just partially, what God has said, and awaken the evil desires of our hearts with the words "Has God indeed said?"

Focusing on these troubling thoughts will eventually cause us to feel distant from God and ashamed before Him. However, we are not without defense against the thoughts of our minds or the tactics of the adversary. Paul says in Ephesians,

> Finally, my brethren, be strong in the Lord and in the power of His might. Put on the whole armor of God, that you may be able to stand against the wiles of the devil. For we do not

wrestle against flesh and blood, but against principalities, against powers, against the rulers of the darkness of this age, against spiritual hosts of wickedness in the heavenly places. (Ephesians 6:10–12)

The Bible says that we must be prepared to stand against the "wiles" of the devil. The Greek word for *wiles* means craft or method, a way of searching after something. The enemy has a fine-tuned method of attack that he has been perfecting for thousands of years, and we *must* be ready to fight against it. But we are far from equipped to do this ourselves. That is precisely why Paul instructs that we suit up with the armor that God provides.

If Jesus promised persecution and Paul spoke of spiritual war, why are so many Christians unprepared when it comes? We often see the armor of God as some cutsie string of verses and do not understand that it is essential to our survival. We think that because we are believers it is automatically on us, not realizing that we must put it on every day, and be ready to fight. It is available to us, but we must choose to put it on. Without God's armor, we are left unequipped and unprepared to engage in war against the enemy. We are left wholly exposed to his fiery arrows, which not only pierce but set ablaze his victims. Peter describes those who are so unprepared for spiritual warfare that they are drawn away from the faith, back to the lives they had before Christ.

For when they speak great swelling words of emptiness, they allure through the lusts of the flesh, through lewdness, the ones who have actually escaped from those who live in error. While they promise them liberty, they themselves are slaves of corruption; for by whom a person is overcome, by him also he is brought into bondage. For if, after they have escaped the pollutions of the world through the knowledge of the Lord and Savior Jesus Christ, they are again entangled in them and overcome, the latter end is worse for them than the beginning. For it would have been better for them not to have known the way of righteousness, than having known it, to turn from the holy commandment delivered to them. But it has happened to them according to the true proverb: "A dog returns to his own vomit," and, "a sow, having washed, to her wallowing in the mire." (2 Peter 2:18–22)

While a true believer cannot fall away or lose his salvation, this warning from Peter should remind the *actual* Christian to war against his flesh and the spiritual forces that press upon him. We must look to those who have gone before us and imitate their endurance in the faith since they have demonstrated battle against persecutions, doubts, and fears (Hebrews 6:9-12 and 11:1-40).

We must be equipped to wage the good warfare with faith in Jesus and a good conscience toward God (1 Timothy 1:18). This is accomplished by putting on Jesus Christ each day, suiting up with the armor of God as we press on toward the prize for the upward call of God in Christ Jesus (Galatians 3:27, Ephesians 4:24, Colossians 3:10–14, 1 Thessalonians 5:8, Philippians 3:12–14).

> Rise each day and fill your spiritual lungs with prayer. Read His Word until you are convicted, encouraged, or instructed. And then find like-minded believers who will sharpen you spiritually.[12]

INTER-ACTUAL EXERCISE:

1. Have you ever experienced what you now recognize as spiritual warfare? How did you handle it when you were faced with this opposition? Is there anything that you would do differently now? Explain why.
2. Significant doubt is not something that is heavily addressed in the church week to week. Do you ever struggle with doubts and fear that God will reject you because of them?
3. How do you prepare for war? As you move forward, will you commit to suiting up in God's armor and finding other believers who will challenge you spiritually as you grow in Christ together?

---

[12] Jack Hibbs, "Watchful," JackHibbs.com. accessed November 21, 2020, https://jackhibbs.com/watchful/.

The night is far spent, the day is at hand. Therefore let us cast off the works of darkness, and let us put on the armor of light. Let us walk properly, as in the day, not in revelry and drunkenness, not in lewdness and lust, not in strife and envy. But put on the Lord Jesus Christ, and make no provision for the flesh, to fulfill its lusts.

—Romans 13:12–14

**Throw off your useless blankets,
seek the Lord, and prepare for war.**

BIBLIOGRAPHY

Bancroft, Charitie Lees. "Before the Throne of God Above." Hymnary.org. Accessed February 20, 2022. https://hymnary.org/text/before_the_throne_of_god_above_i_have_a_.

Crosby, Fanny. "To God Be The Glory." Hymnary.org. Accessed February 20, 2022. https://hymnary.org/text/to_god_be_the_glory_great_things_he_hath.

Henry, Matthew. "Matthew Henry's Commentary—Verses 6–9." BibleGateway.com. Accessed July 28, 2022. https://www.biblegateway.com/resources/matthew-henry/Luke.13.6-Luke.13.9.

Hibbs, Jack. "Watchful." JackHibbs.com. Accessed November 21, 2020. https://jackhibbs.com/watchful/.

McGee, J. Vernon. *Romans*. Nashville, TN: T. Nelson, 1991.

Owen, John. *The Nature, Power, Deceit, and Prevalency*. London: Cockerill, 1675.

Smart, Susan. "Charles Blondin Story—Faith on a Tightrope." CreativeBibleStudy.com. Accessed February 21, 2022. https://www.creativeBiblestudy.com/Blondin-story.html.

Ten Boom, Corrie. "Corrie Ten Boom: Quotable Quote." Goodreads.com. Accessed March 4, 2022. https://www.goodreads.com/quotes/51450-trying-to-do-the-lord-s-work-in-your-own-strength.

Tozer, A. W. *Man—the Dwelling Place of God*. Blacksburg, VA: Wilder Publications, 2009.

———. *The Pursuit of God: The Human Thirst for the Divine*. Chicago, IL: Moody Publishers, 2015.

ABOUT THE AUTHOR

Matthew Braden is a dedicated six-year student of God's Word. His education began at the church he attends regularly today. He obtained a bachelor's degree in business from Towson University in 2019 and went on to pursue more Bible-centered education through Men with a Mission, a three-year intensive discipleship class led by Pastor Wally Webster. The program equips men to properly exegete the Scriptures and trains them to become effective disciple-makers in the community and leaders in the church. At Mount Airy Bible Church (MABC), Matthew consistently serves in the music ministry and teaches adult Sunday school classes on various topics.

Matthew has authored this first book with one goal in mind: to help others see their true and total need for Jesus. His desire to see others receive Christ is driven by his own story filled with confusion, doubt, and questioning. Matthew grew up attending MABC and eventually came to a place where he questioned his faith and Christianity as a whole. Since then, Matthew has sought out the truth about God and His Word and has come to know the Lord in a true and personal way. In his writing, Matthew presents the truth of God's Word through deep study and meticulous exegesis in the hopes of introducing his readers to the one, true, and living God.

Printed in the United States
by Baker & Taylor Publisher Services